My Cat's Tale

By Lorie Glantz
with Amy D. Shojai

Illustrations by Emily Youngreen

Delacorte

Illustrations on pages 17, 19, 23, 59, 71, and 101 by Pat Cheal
All other illustrations by Emily Youngreen

Published by
Delacorte Press
Random House, Inc.
1540 Broadway
New York, New York 10036

Delacorte Press® is a registered trademark
of Random House, Inc., and the colophon
is a trademark of Random House, Inc.

ISBN 0-385-33539-3

Manufactured in the United States of America.
Published simultaneously in Canada.
October 2000

10 9 8 7 6 5 4 3 2 1
RRH

DEDICATION

To Tom, Lucille, Nolan, and Zachary

ACKNOWLEDGMENTS

To my parents, you have been fundamental in the journey of my life. To Nolan, thank you for your love, faith, and all of your hard work. To Max and Marcia, your counsel was invaluable. To my grandmother Katherine, you have always made me feel special and loved. Thank you for all that you have done for me. Last but not least, to my son Zachary, I am so glad our journey together has just begun.

To Glen Edelstein, thank you for helping this book stay on course. A sincere thanks to Larry Wengren and all my alpha readers for reviewing my manuscripts. To Holly Webber of HDW Enterprises, thank you for letting me use your feline fun facts. A special thanks to Emily Youngreen and Pat Cheal whose wonderful illustrations grace the pages of this book. Emily, thank you for breathing life into my thoughts. To Joel Avirom, your talent is clearly seen in the design of this book. To my agent, Meredith Bernstein, thank you for seeing my vision and teaching me by example. To my editor, Danielle Perez, who helped me along the bumpy road of publication and has answered my endless list of questions, I thank you for your understanding.

This book is a journal of the life and times of my cat

. . . .

I began creating this journal on

. . . .

If for any reason this journal gets lost,
please contact me at:

. . . .

. . . .

Kitten's Birthday

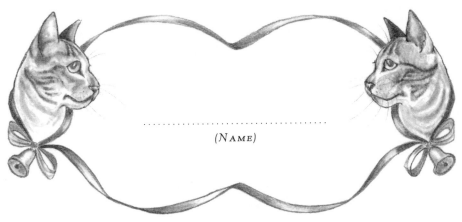

....

(Name)

Was born on

....

In the year

....

At birth our kitten weighed

....

(lbs./ozs.)

Our kitten is a

....

(boy/girl)

and is a

....

(breed)

Time spent with cats is never wasted.

—COLETTE

My Cat's Tale is a journal of many things. Most importantly, it is a journal of your incredible relationship with your cat. In tracking the everyday events and the milestones that shape your cat's life, you create a permanent document that honors and cherishes the bond you have with your cat. It is my greatest hope that creating this journal will give you joy and enrich your relationship with your cat.

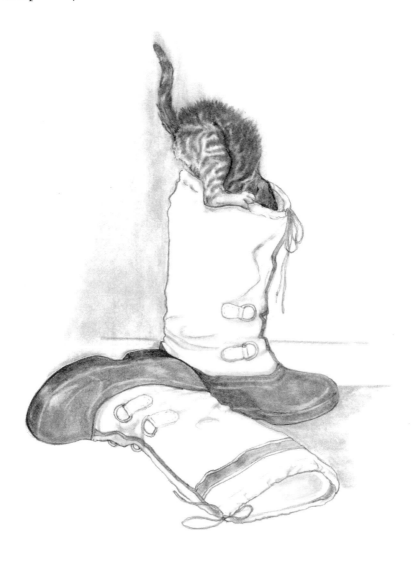

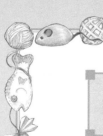

FAVORITE KITTY PICTURES

Adopting a New Family Member

Congratulations! By the time you are reading this, you probably have decided to adopt a cat or are living with one already. By doing this, you have made a decision to extend your family, which now includes a wonderful feline that will add tremendous joy to your life. With this enjoyment comes responsibility and hard work. For most of us, all the hard work pales in comparison with the love and spiritual nourishment that we get from our relationships with our cats.

The bonds we have with our cats are rewardingly comforting and pure. There are few relationships in life that can match the ones we have with our cats. They possess the ability to lift our spirits, to share our deepest secrets, and to make us laugh.

Life just seems better when you share it with a cat. Cats seem to have a way of bringing out the best in us—somehow we are more human when we are with them. Whether you have experienced these feelings yet or not, one thing is for sure—you are about to embark upon a journey that will change and shape your life in powerful ways, ways that you cannot even imagine.

Cat Nip: Scenting of an Object

If you get your cat from a breeder, before you bring your cat home, take a soft toy or towel to the breeder's. Have the breeder leave the item with the litter to get the scent of the mother and siblings on it. If you get your cat from a shelter or another source, try to bring home something from the cat's previous residence. A familiar scent will make the transition for the cat much easier. Place this object in the cat's area in your home.

Choosing a Name

Choosing a name for the new member of your family is a very personal and important decision. This process can be fun and frustrating at the same time. The bottom line is, pick a name that you like.

Tips for Choosing a Name

- It is best to keep the call name, the name you will use every day for the cat, to one or two syllables.

- Beginning the name with a hard consonant is a good idea because cats tend to hear consonants more readily.

- Generate names associated with the place where you got your cat (e.g., name of town or state). If you found your cat, try conceiving names related to the type of place where you found your cat.

- Think of themes that are important in your life (e.g., the outdoors, sports, or music); then generate a list of words that you associate with those themes.

- If you decide on the name of your kitten before you actually get her, give the name that you choose time to settle in. Even say it out loud to see how it sounds.

- If you don't decide on a name before you get your kitten, you may be able to generate some ideas for a name based on the kitten's personality or markings.

The Kitten's Name

WE NAMED OUR KITTEN

. . . .

ON

. . . .

HOW WE CHOSE OUR KITTEN'S NAME

. . . .

. . . .

. . . .

THE SPECIAL SIGNIFICANCE OF OUR KITTEN'S NAME

. . . .

. . . .

. . . .

OTHER NAMES THAT WE CONSIDERED

. . . .

. . . .

Cat Nip: Naming Concerns

Try to pick a name that doesn't sound similar to either a word that is used often in normal conversation or a command you would give your cat. Cats respond better to names that start in a consonant and end in an "ee" sound.

LITTER MATES

Kitten's name . . . .
Gender . . . .
Owner's name . . . .
Address . . . .

. . . .
Phone . . . .
E-mail address . . . .

Kitten's name . . . .
Gender . . . .
Owner's name . . . .
Address . . . .

. . . .
Phone . . . .
E-mail address . . . .

Kitten's name . . . .
Gender . . . .
Owner's name . . . .
Address . . . .

. . . .
Phone . . . .
E-mail address . . . .

Kitten's name . . . .
Gender . . . .
Owner's name . . . .
Address . . . .

. . . .
Phone . . . .
E-mail address . . . .

Kitten's name . . . .
Gender . . . .
Owner's name . . . .
Address . . . .

. . . .
Phone . . . .
E-mail address . . . .

Kitten's name . . . .
Gender . . . .
Owner's name . . . .
Address . . . .

. . . .
Phone . . . .
E-mail address . . . .

FELINE FAMILY TREE

OUR CAT

....
Name

....
Date of Birth

....
Breed

MOTHER

....
Name

....
Date of Birth

....
Breed

....
Owner

....
Address

....
Phone

....
E-Mail

FATHER

....
Name

....
Date of Birth

....
Breed

....
Owner

....
Address

....
Phone

....
E-Mail

Preparations Before Bringing Home a Kitten

KITTEN-PROOFING

LIKE ALL BABIES, CURIOUS KITTENS get into all kinds of mischief—from simply aggravating to downright dangerous. Before you bring home the new kitty, it's vital that you kitten-proof your house. If the kitten spends any time outside, you must also consider the yard and the garage.

The ideal way to kitten-proof is to invest in kneepads and crawl around the house and yard at kitten eye level (if you're up to it). But don't neglect second-story opportunities; cats love to climb, the higher the better. They love small warm cubbyholes, so block off dangerous openings and check countertops. Any object that swings, sways, or can be swatted is fair game to be clawed or bitten. Move them out of reach, or immobilize the movement to make them less tempting play objects.

KITTEN-PROOFING CHECKLIST

The House

- Secure cleaning products, chemicals, and medications, especially in your kitchen and bathroom.

- Place wastebaskets and recycling containers out of reach.

- Tape electrical cords (TV, VCR, lamps, stereo, computer, appliances, etc.) to baseboards, or paint with a noxious cat repellent product like Bitter Apple®.

- Tie cords from drapes and blinds out of reach; tie back drapes and raise blinds.

- Keep sewing supplies (yarn, thread, needles) and office supplies (staples, paperclips) in a cat-proof cabinet.

- Keep appliance (dishwashers, washers, dryers, ovens) doors shut, and always check inside before starting.

- Place covers over the burners on the stovetop.

- Block off the flue in chimneys and/or install cat-proof fire screens.

- Clear tabletops, shelves, and countertops of sharp and breakable objects.

- Block off balcony railings.

The Garage

- Tape closed any unused stray boxes, and store containers of tools, nails, or fishing supplies (hooks, feather lures, fishing line, etc.) in a secure place.

- Cats like to sleep under car hoods; bang on the hood and/or honk the horn before starting the car.

- Secure any chemicals or toxic compounds, including paint, rat poison, and antifreeze.

The Yard

- Kittens escape through tiny holes or can climb over the fence. Cat Fence-In systems, available through mail-order catalogs, are netting products that attach to the tops of existing permanent boundaries (fences, trees, shed roofs) to contain cats safely.

- Are the pool and/or hot tub safe? Though they can swim, kittens unable to climb out of the water can drown.

- Secure pool chemicals in a safe place, and check the safety of storage sheds.

- What about trees? Kittens that climb very high will risk falls and broken bones.

- Do you have any dangerous plants?

You may not be aware that many common houseplants or yard plants can be toxic or even fatal to kittens. They don't have to eat it to be affected; kittens and cats tend to bat leaves in play, and when they lick off their claws, they are exposed. If you are not sure whether a plant or compound is poisonous to your cat, call your vet or the ASPCA National Animal Poison Control Center. Consultations can be charged to your credit card by calling 1-800-548-2423 or to your phone bill at 1-900-680-0000. The list below is a partial list of problem plants (*The Purina Encyclopedia of Cat Care*, Amy D. Shojai, 1998).

Toxic Plants, Trees, and Shrubs

Azalea

Chrysanthemum

Dieffenbachia (dumb cane)

English ivy

Holly

Hydrangea

Iris

Lily of the valley

Morning glory

Oleander

Philodendron (heart-leaf and split-leaf)

Potato (green parts and eyes)

Rhubarb (upper stem and leaves)

Weeping fig

Yew

Toxic Seeds and Pits

Apple seeds

Apricot pits

Cherry pits

Peach pits

Toxic Bulbs

Daffodil

Tulip

Wisteria

Essential Supplies

It's best to have these supplies on hand and set up before the kitten arrives. That way you can enjoy and keep an eye on the kitten as you introduce him to your home.

Kitten Food Choose a product that is formulated specifically for kittens, and use it for a full year because muscles, nerves, and emotions continue to develop until kittens are 12 to 14 months old.

Commercial products are available in either canned or dry form. Feed the baby three to four times a day, and reduce to twice-daily feedings once he reaches six months. Kittens less than ten weeks old may not be able to eat dry food at first—you can soften it with warm water and slowly reduce the amount of moisture until he accepts dry. Cow's milk is hard for kittens to digest and will give them diarrhea.

Dishes All kinds of commercial cat dishes are available. If you plan to feed both canned and dry food, use a dish for each, plus a bowl for water. For food, a saucer style, made of glass or ceramic, works best. Dishes must be easily washed to remove old food smells that turn off the cat's appetite. Plastic dishes are often hard to clean, and some cats get allergic reactions to them and develop acne on their chins.

Litter Box and Fillers The litter box is your kitten's bathroom. Make it so attractive that there's never any question that he'll use it. The facilities should be large enough that he can turn around inside without problems, but not so large that he can't see over the sides. Tiny kittens may need help at first getting into the pan. Pans must be deep enough to hold at least two inches of filler, but not so shallow that digging kicks it out of the box.

The box filler is as important as the container. Cats are concerned about odor and texture. Clay-based products are the most popular. The best choice is one your

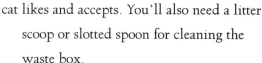

Cat Nip: Kitty Dishes

Choose dishes that are heavy enough that the cat won't push them around the room when he eats. Shallow wide dishes are best—cats dislike diving into a deep bowl because they can't see out, and they get food all over themselves. They also hate getting their whiskers bent.

cat likes and accepts. You'll also need a litter scoop or slotted spoon for cleaning the waste box.

Scratching Object Scratching is natural cat behavior that cannot be eliminated. Instead, provide an outlet for the inevitable. Commercial scratching objects are available in a wide range of styles. Make sure it's tall enough or long enough that he can really stretch out to give claws a workout.

Identification A collar with an ID tag provides contact information so he can be safely returned if he's ever lost. Many city shelters now also provide microchip identification. A tiny glass capsule with encoded computer information is implanted painlessly beneath the kitten's skin, so you can be reunited if he's ever lost.

Grooming Tools Pick up a Teflon-coated flea comb (the Teflon keeps it from sticking or breaking hairs) with the tines very close together for shorthaired kittens. A curry or slicker brush works well for longer-haired kittens.

Cat Nip: Scratching Choices

Look for a style that the kitten can sink his claws into—those covered with carpet, upholstery fabric, or sisal are big hits with most cats. Vertical styles must be stable so they don't tip over when the kitten scratches. Some cats prefer horizontal styles they can lie on and dig into.

Highly Suggested Supplies

Carrier Every cat will travel at some point in his life, if only to the veterinarian for a checkup—a kitty carrier will provide comfort and safety. Hard carriers made of plastic have a wire grill front or top opening. Duffel-style cases are soft fabric with zipper mesh openings and can double as a bed.

Toys Provide lots of toys for your new kitten. Like any youngster, kittens get easily bored so you'll want an assortment. Keep three to five out at all times, and rotate them a couple of times a week to keep the kitten interested.

Leash and Harness When your kitten will walk on a leash, it opens up all sorts of opportunities for him to travel safely with you. Choose a figure-eight cat harness that won't slip off the wiggly baby or put pressure on his delicate neck.

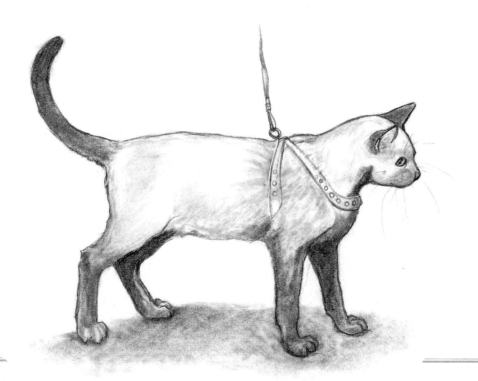

Catnip Catnip is a relative of the mint plant, and the scent goes straight to the kitty's pleasure center in the brain and produces a harmless feline "high." Kittens tend not to react too strongly to catnip before they're about six months old.

Bed Kittens and cats spend lots of time asleep—and they may not be particular where. But many stylish cat beds are available, from tunnels and bags to cozy cushions and hammocks. And if your kitten develops an allegiance to his own bed, you won't have to fight him for the covers!

More Grooming Tools

- Cat-safe shampoo

- Eye stain remover

- Ear-cleaning solution

- Hairball medicine

- Chamois cloth

- Nail trimmer

- Cat toothpaste and finger toothbrush

Cat Tree A cat tree provides lots of opportunity for the kitten to climb and scratch and become king of all he surveys. A cat tree is important, especially in homes that have limited space because cats will relish the vertical space.

Cat Nip: The Thrill of the Nip

Technically called Nepeta cataria, catnip affects all members of the cat family, including lions and tigers. But the tendency to react to catnip is inherited—the kitty must have the right "genes" to be affected. About one-third of cats won't ever know or care about the thrill of catnip.

Questions to Ask Before the Kitten Moves In

What's Your Lifestyle?

KITTENS AND CATS ARE HIGHLY ADAPTABLE. But you can't turn the cat on and off like a light switch—kittens will be "on" whether you're there to supervise or not. And the more time you spend with the furry baby, the closer you'll bond and the better pet he'll become. So consider how you'll meet the emotional and health care needs of your kitten:

- Do you work at home? Can you get work done with a kitten underfoot?

- Do you leave the house several hours a day? Will the kitten be safe alone while you're at work?

- Can you stand to have furniture or cherished knickknacks rearranged or even broken? Kittens tend to redecorate.

- Do you live alone? Who will care for the kitten if you need to leave town?

- Do you share the house with a spouse? It is essential your spouse support the decision to get a pet!

- Have children? How old are the children? Will you have time to attend to your human babies' needs, teach the children about the kitten, and care for furry baby, too?

Cat Nip: Searching for the Correct Kitty

Acquire pedigree kittens only from responsible, respected breeders—pet shop kittens tend to have a questionable heritage and health. Nonpedigree kittens are available from friends, from shelters, or as strays.

CARE AND TEMPERAMENT

All kittens potentially make great pets, but certain characteristics can help you predict temperament and care requirements:

- Shorthaired cats take less coat care than longhaired varieties. Breeds like Persians that have long double coats need a half-hour combing every day!

- Nonpedigree kittens are the most popular type of pet cat, but certain breeds may have a more predictable temperament. For instance, a Persian tends to be easygoing and laid back. A Siamese "talks" a lot and tends to bond strongly to one family member. The Abyssinian is a nonstop action figure that runs and leaps and lounges on door tops.

OTHER CONSIDERATIONS

- Decide who will be the primary caretaker.

- Choose a veterinarian.

- Decide where the kitten will live. Exclusively indoors? Some outdoor privileges? Stay exclusively outdoors? Cats allowed to roam outside unsupervised are exposed to that which can cut their life short, while indoor cats tend to live longer, healthier lives.

- Evaluate spay and neuter considerations. All nonpedigree kittens should be sterilized; consult with the kitten's breeder to see if pedigree kittens should be included in a responsible breeding program.

- Estimate the cost of the kitten—above and beyond the purchase price.

> ## Cat Nip:
> ## First Car Ride Home
>
> *Transport the kitten home in a carrier.*

Kitten's First Day Home

TODAY

. . . .

WE ADOPTED OUR NEW KITTEN

. . . .

During the car ride home, our kitten . . . .

. . . .

. . . .

. . . .

. . . .

I will never forget . . . .

. . . .

. . . .

. . . .

. . . .

. . . .

. . . .

. . . .

. . . .

. . . .

Some of the things we did that day were . . . .
. . . .
. . . .
. . . .
. . . .
. . . .
. . . .
. . . .
. . . .
. . . .
. . . .

Cat Nip: First Day

Keep your kitten's first few days at home quiet; wait a few days to have guests over. Let the kitten explore her new surroundings while you follow behind her. Do not let her roam around the house alone. You need to watch the kitten in order to keep her out of trouble. Expect her to take several naps; have a safe area for this, either in a carrier or in a safe room (e.g., laundry room or bathroom). Having the kitten sleep in a carrier in the kitchen allows the kitty to get used to the sounds of daily activity.

Kitten's First Night Home

We fell asleep . . . .
. . . .
. . . .
. . . .
. . . .
. . . .

During the night the kitten . . . .
. . . .
. . . .
. . . .
. . . .
. . . .

The next morning . . . .
. . . .
. . . .
. . . .
. . . .
. . . .

Cat Nip: First Night

Your kitten should spend the night in a kitten-proofed room that contains food, water, a litter box, and toys. This can be your bedroom, but beware the kitty may keep you up half the night. If you had the chance to get an object from the kitten's previous residence, place it in the room with the kitty.

THE EARLY DAYS

Left Front Paw

Right Front Paw

Left Rear Paw

Right Rear Paw

DATE:

IDENTIFICATION MARKS

Color of eyes . . . .

Color of coat . . . .

Any distinguishing marks or colorings . . . .

. . . .

. . . .

MAKING THE PAW PRINTS

Be aware that this could get a bit messy, and you might get some scratches. Lay down newspapers before you begin. Get a bowl of warm soapy water, and have some old towels close by. Take a standard ink pad, in the color of your choice, and place your cat's paw firmly on the ink pad. Then carefully place your cat's paw in the center of the appropriate square. After you're done with each paw, dip the paw in the soapy water and wipe it off. This can be quite a challenging project—so good luck!

Cat Nip: The Toe Count

The cat's front paws have five toes, but the back paws have four toes. Some cats are born with as many as seven front toes and even more back toes—this is called polydactyl.

Litter Box Training

Bathroom Behavior

Cats are fastidious creatures that want to keep their homes clean. Burying waste is a natural behavior that kittens learned from watching and imitating their mothers. They also cover up feces and urine to show their submission to older or more dominant individuals.

In most instances, all you'll need to do to train your kitten to use the litter box is point out the location, place the kitten in the box, and let him watch as you scratch your fingers through the litter. If he has an accident elsewhere, deposit the sample in the box so he'll have a scent cue to prompt the behavior. Praise the kitty when he's productive.

Litter Box Guidelines

If the kitten hasn't used the box consistently, there could be several reasons. Usually it's easy to fix the problem by following a few guidelines:

Style of Box Size of the box may not be a problem with small kittens, but large ones may outgrow the facilities and "let it all hang out" by accident. Other cats may prefer the privacy of the potted palm rather than an open box. A covered box or even a privacy screen will hide the cat in action from intruding eyes.

Type of Filler Strongly perfumed litters can be offensive because the feline sense of smell is so sensitive, and that can prompt cats to find other facilities. Dusty fillers may make it uncomfortable for the kitten to breathe. When you find a product your cat likes and uses, stick with it.

Location of Box Like real estate, location is everything. Place the litter box in a low-traffic area, and make sure the feeding station is some distance away. Cats don't want to eliminate near where they eat.

Make sure a new kitten knows where he can find the box. Place him in the litter box, let him do his business, and then allow him to leave and follow you back into the house so he'll learn the route.

It may be necessary to have more than one box strategically placed in both ends of the house, or one upstairs and one downstairs. Some cats refuse to use a box after another cat has used it. Multicat homes should provide one litter box for each cat.

Timing Is Everything Bodily functions can be predicted with young kittens by paying attention to eating, sleeping, and playing patterns. About 15 minutes after eating or waking, or immediately after an energetic play period, give the kitten an opportunity to use the box.

Cleanliness Is Key Nothing will prompt a cat to boycott the box faster than filthy facilities. Keep the waste material cleaned out religiously—at least once a day, and more often if you have more than one cat. Plain clay litters and some other types will require you to dump the entire box every week. "Clumping" litters that congeal liquid into solid balls allow you to scoop only the waste and leave clean litter behind; you'll still need to dump the entire box every two to four weeks. Scrub the plastic with warm water and soap, dry it thoroughly, and if you like, spray it with alcohol to disinfect. Again, dry the box thoroughly before filling with new, clean litter. Do not use any commercial cleaning products that contain phenol (like Lysol®) to clean litter-boxes, as these tend to be highly toxic to cats.

STARTING OFF ON THE RIGHT PAW

SOCIALIZATION

KITTENS MUST BE PROPERLY SOCIALIZED if they are to reach their full potential as pets. Introduce kittens to strange situations, friendly people, and other dogs or cats so that when they grow up, they will be more accepting. Make sure your furry baby is exposed to a wide range of experiences, like riding in a carrier or taking a bath. Make these positive, happy events whenever possible so he'll accept them more readily.

GENERAL HEALTH

The best way to keep your kitten healthy is to learn to recognize what's normal—and what's not. That way you can get help promptly if you notice something's wrong.

A healthy kitten has:

- Boundless energy and curiosity
- Good appetite
- Sleek short haircoat or fluffy fur
- No bald patches or scaly scabby skin
- No parasites (such as fleas)
- Bright, clear eyes without a discharge
- Clean ears
- Nose that isn't runny
- Clean bottom with no evidence of diarrhea

Protect your kitten with routine preventive care provided by your veterinarian. Cat lifestyle also impacts what preventive care is necessary. For instance, an "only" cat kept exclusively indoors won't be exposed to the same things as an outdoor cat that roams and meets strange kitties. Your veterinarian can advise you on the specific health care measures that are best for your baby. Here are the basic care considerations for kittens.

Parasites Kittens may carry all kinds of buggy freeloaders that live off them and make them sick. Common problems include:

- Roundworms
- Giardia
- Hookworms
- Coccidiosis

- Tapeworms
- Fleas and ticks
- Ear mites
- Heartworms (carried by mosquitoes)

Elective Surgery Unless your kitten is a registered purebred, he should be surgically altered to prevent reproduction. The American Veterinary Medical Association endorses spaying and neutering kittens from shelters at four months. This prevents many obnoxious behaviors, prevents certain health problems, and makes your kitten a much happier and more well-adjusted pet.

Cat Nip: Just the Paw Facts

- *Cats sweat from the pads of their paws.*
- *Cats walk on their toes.*
- *Cats step with both left legs, then both right legs when they walk or run.*

CAT BEHAVIORS

IT'S IMPORTANT TO RECOGNIZE normal cat behavior so that you better understand your kitten. A sudden change in behavior is a red flag warning you that there may be a health or emotional problem and to see your veterinarian.

Cat Nip: Will Cats Always Land on Their Feet?

Although this is a common belief, it is a myth.

SECOND-STORY EXPERTS

Cats love high places. Claws are used as grappling hooks to climb aloft, but cats also can leap incredible heights. Tree-climbing cats may be reluctant to come down on their own—their claws curve the wrong way, so using them effectively would mean descending backward in a decidedly uncatlike way.

MARKING BEHAVIOR

Cats are territorial creatures that mark their property to claim ownership.

Spraying Older male cats and some females spray urine in a standing position to mark objects with the scent. Neutering usually eliminates the behavior.

Rubbing Cats have scent glands in their cheeks, chins, and tails and often rub against objects. Twining around your ankle and head-bumping your face (called bunting) are huge compliments—the cat is marking you as his personal territory so that you belong to him.

Scratching Scent glands in the paw pads leave their signature odor behind whenever the cat scratches an object. Cats also use the visible scratch marks as cues.

Seeing Is Believing

Every two months for the kitten's first year, take a photograph of your kitty with the same toy. Take the picture in the same place each time. Make sure that you always stand about four feet away from your kitten when you take each of the pictures. When you take the photograph, either kneel down or sit down on the ground; you want to be eye level with your kitten. After one year, you will have a visual growth chart for your cat, and you will also be able to see how your cat's toy stands the test of time.

Note: Plan to crop the photos to fit them all on the next two pages.

Height Growth Chart

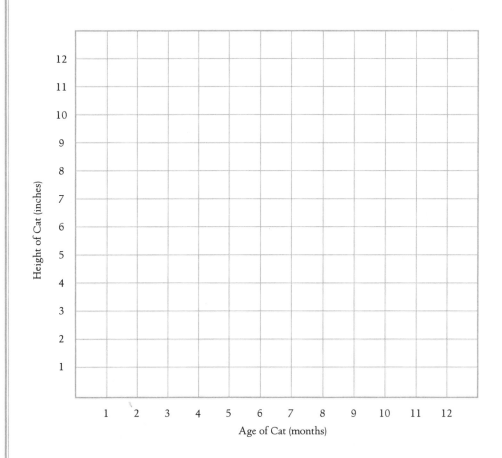

Height of Cat (inches)

Age of Cat (months)

Cat Nip: How High Can a Kitty Pounce?

A cat can jump five times as high as it is tall.

WEIGHT GAIN CHART

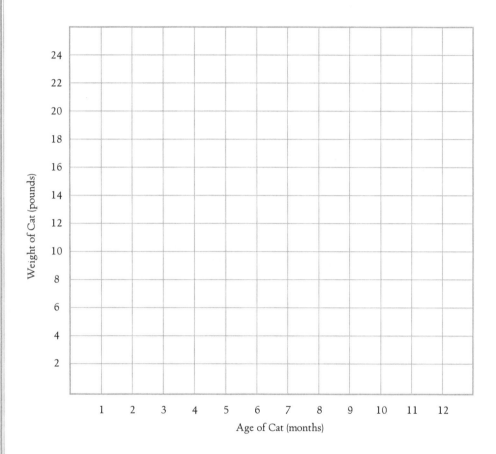

Weight of Cat (pounds)

24
22
20
18
16
14
12
10
8
6
4
2

1   2   3   4   5   6   7   8   9   10   11   12

Age of Cat (months)

Cat Nip: How to Tell If You Have a Fat Cat

Place your hands on both sides of your cat's rib cage. Rub your hands back and forth over your cat's ribs. You should be able to feel the ribs easily, without applying too much pressure. Overweight cats tend to carry a "pouch" of fat under their tummy between their rear legs, even though you might be able to feel their ribs. This is just a guideline—before restricting your cat's diet, consult your veterinarian.

GROOMING: *A Lick* AND A *Promise*

CATS USE THEIR TONGUES LIKE A COMB to smooth the fur and clean off dirt; they nibble with their teeth to prevent tangles and to scratch places that are hard to reach with rear claws. They use a dampened forepaw like a washcloth to clean their faces. Grooming maintains healthy skin by catching parasites and massaging the body.

Despite this dedication to cleanliness, cats need your help to keep their fur—and the rest of their bodies—in the best condition possible. By self-grooming, cats tend to swallow shed fur, and that can cause hairballs. Regular combing and brushing can reduce or even eliminate hairballs.

Fur Care Shorthaired cats do a good job of keeping their coats clean. When needed, a rubber curry brush works great to remove loose fur. Longhaired cats need regular combing to prevent painful mats from developing. Breeds like Persians tend to mat in the "armpit" and "groin" areas. Comb longhaired cats two to three times a week (Persians need daily attention). A wire slicker brush or a pin brush reaches through thick, long fur.

Bathing All cats may benefit from an occasional dunking. Rushing water and unfamiliar sights, sounds, and smells scare cats and can make the experience unpleasant. Have warm water (102 degrees) ready in the sink, set the kitten in the water only to soak him, then set him on a towel to apply pet shampoo designed specifically for kittens. Avoid dog products, people shampoos, and dishwashing detergents—they can be dangerous! Set the kitten back into the water to rinse thoroughly, and be sure to completely dry him in a towel so he doesn't chill.

Nail Care   Cat claws can catch in carpeting and upholstery. For kittens, you can use regular people nail trimmers or invest in pet nail trimmers. Trim just the sharp hook off the ends to avoid cutting the "quick" (the blood vessel in the nail) that will bleed. If you do cut the quick, put some Kwik Stop® on the nail to stop the bleeding. Trimming once a week will keep claws in fine shape.

Eyes and Ears   Flat-faced breeds like Persians tend to have big prominent eyes that water, and the tears can crust or stain the fur. To prevent this problem, soak a cotton ball in warm water or saline solution to wipe away excess tears each day. Commercial products work to remove fur stains beneath the eyes.

Check the insides of the ears every week. Place a bit of mineral oil on a cotton ball to swab out visible areas. Any dark discharge or crumbly material should be checked by a veterinarian to rule out parasites.

Dental Care   Use a soft baby toothbrush or one designed specifically for cats. There are cat toothpaste products flavored like fish or chicken that many cats love. Don't use human toothpaste products—the fluoride can be dangerous for them. Ideally, clean your kitten's teeth after every meal or at least once or twice a week.

Cat Nip: Grooming Habits

Kittens start to groom themselves at two weeks of age. Cats spend up to 50 percent of their awake time grooming themselves.

The First Bath

Cat Nip: Bathing

Wash the kitten's face with a washcloth to avoid getting
water or soap in his eyes or ears. Also, place a towel,
window screen, or plastic milk carton in the bottom of
the sink or tub to give kitty something besides your arm
to claw and cling to during the bath.

Date: . . . .

My kitten's first bath . . . .
. . . .
. . . .
. . . .
. . . .
. . . .

Memorable Firsts

First car trip. . . . .
. . . .
. . . .
. . . .
. . . .
. . . .

First trip to vet. . . . .
. . . .
. . . .
. . . .
. . . .
. . . .
. . . .

First "kill". . . . .
. . . .
. . . .
. . . .
. . . .
. . . .
. . . .

First catnip experience . . . .
. . . .
. . . .
. . . .
. . . .
. . . .

First trip up the stairs. . . . .
. . . .
. . . .
. . . .
. . . .
. . . .

First "gravity experiment" . . . .
. . . .
. . . .
. . . .
. . . .
. . . .

First . . . .
. . . .
. . . .
. . . .
. . . .
. . . .

UNDERSTANDING KITTY LANGUAGE

How Cats Communicate

PEOPLE ARE VERY VOCAL CREATURES, and we expect cats to communicate the same way. However, vocalizations are only a small part of your kitten's language. Cats also communicate with scent signals and with sounds that are so quiet we can't hear them.

Vocalizations

- Murmur patterns include purrs and trills, and they indicate contentment and happiness.

- Vowel patterns can be a variety of meows used to request or demand something—like to be fed or to go in or out. Typically, the more agitated the cat, the lower the pitch of the meow.

- Articulated patterns express frustration or solicitation and include chirping or chattering sounds. Cats do this when they can't reach that tantalizing bird outside the window.

- Strained intensity sounds include spits, hisses, growls, and screams and are used in attack, defense, and mating. They warn other animals or people to stay away.

Cat Nip: Kitty Talk

Cats have about 100 different vocalization sounds. In comparison, dogs only have about 10 vocalization sounds.

Body Language Cats speak to us in very subtle ways. To understand what they're saying, each part of the body must be "read" and then put together in context:

- Body Talk Kittens show they trust and love you by putting themselves in vulnerable positions like lying on their backs or sleeping with their tail toward you. Confident cats meet you head-on. Fearful cats turn sideways and arch their backs to look as big as possible. And cats cry "uncle" by crouching as low to the ground as they can.

- Whisker Talk When fanned straight out or forward, whiskers show interest and happiness. They are drawn tight against the face when kitty is fearful or upset.

- Tail Talk A tail held straight up—sometimes with just the end tipped over—is a greeting. A content, happy cat's tail curves down in a gentle U shape. Tail tips twitch when the cat feels frustration—this is used to warn. Tail flicks escalate to tail flailings or thumpings when kitty becomes upset and are often followed by claws or an attack. A fluffed tail held straight out shows aggression, but tails fluffed and held in an inverted U mean the cat is scared.

- **Ear Talk** Interested cats hold their ears facing forward. Ears turn to the side and press flat against the head by degrees as cats feel threatened, fearful, or angry.

- **Eye Talk** Droopy eyelids show trust, wide eyes show alertness, and an unblinking stare shows dominance and aggression. Any strong emotion causes a sudden contraction of the cat's pupils.

- **Fur Talk** When happy and content, the fur lies close to the body. Cats fluff their fur to show aggression or fear—it makes them look bigger so they can "bluff" their enemies to go away.

> ## Cat Nip: Ear Power
>
> *A cat has over 19 muscles in each ear.*

The Feline Mind

Feline Social Structure

- The cat considers himself king. He wants all the best resting spots or the tastiest food, and to be petted on demand—until a bigger, more powerful cat (or person) puts him in his place. Even then, kitty will only acknowledge the superior individual when that person or other animal is nearby.

- Cats are incredibly attuned to place and territory. Feline dynamics within a social group are fluid and change according to which individuals are present. They also change depending on the location. That means that one cat may be king when he's upstairs, but another cat is the ruler on the first floor.

- Cats are incredibly smart. Cats learn very quickly what's allowed and what's not—and how to get around the rules to do exactly what they want. Your job is to outthink your kitten from the beginning and be the biggest, smartest King Cat in your house.

Cat Nip: The Feline Brain

A cat's brain is more similar to a human's brain than to that of a dog. Both humans and cats have identical regions in the brain responsible for emotions.

Kitty Boot Camp

CATS HAVE A REPUTATION FOR BEING "untrainable," but actually cats are trained from the moment they arrive as kittens in your home. For instance, a cat quickly learns where to find his food bowl.

Focus from the beginning on the rules of the house, and remain consistent. Give kitty every opportunity to be good by removing temptations from reach and making the right choice also the easiest choice.

TRAINING BASICS

■ Voice commands and physical direction should always be conducted in a matter-of-fact way. Raising your voice only communicates anger and doesn't help the training process.

■ Train in short five-minute sessions several times a day. Kittens have a short attention span. Keep things pleasant, and end the sessions with something fun like a game.

■ Cats tend to be food-oriented or toy-oriented and can be bribed to use good behavior or can be rewarded when they do something right.

■ Identify bribes and rewards with a key word, phrase, or signal. For example, always say "Good kitty!" or use a clicker (the Halloween "crickets") as you offer the treat or toy. Eventually kitty learns that just the phrase or signal means he's done something right.

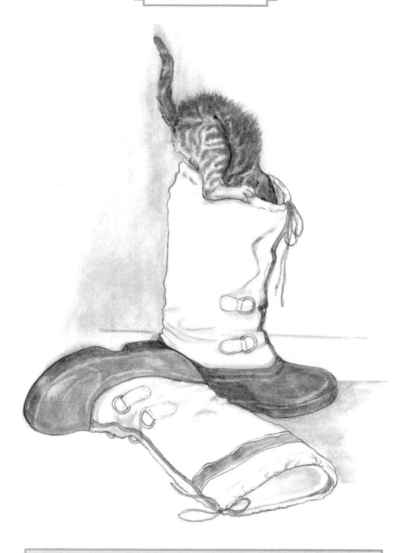

Cat Nip: Creating a Stronger Bond with Your Cat

Talking out loud to your kitten on a regular basis helps him
bond more closely to you so he is more willing to please you, pays
attention to your voice, and is easier to train.

KITTY COMMANDS

BELOW ARE SOME VERY USEFUL COMMANDS to teach your cat. Teaching your cat these commands can make your life together much more enjoyable and safer.

Important Commands

- *"Off"*—Cats like high places, but some perches may be dangerous for them, like the stovetop, or undesirable for you, like the dining room table. Give the command "Off" in your normal voice, and entice the kitten down with a treat. Give the treat once he's off the forbidden area.

- *"Come"*—This is one of the most important commands because coming on command could save your cat's life. Let the cat's dinnertime double as a training session. Cats tend to run whenever they hear the "whirrrrrr" of the can opener or crackle of the kibble bag. As you fill the bowl and before kitty makes his appearance, give the "Come" command in your normal voice. And when he appears, present him with the food. Eventually, kitty will come whenever called even if there's no treat because there just might be a treat!

Fun Commands

You can easily train cats to perform natural behaviors on command simply by naming the action and rewarding it.

- *"Sit"*—Place the cat on a table and stand in front of him. Show him the treat or toy, and move it slowly up and over his head. To keep his balance while he watches, he'll have to sit—time your command "Sit" so that you say the word just as his tail hits the table. Reward with lots of praise and the treat.

- "*Wave*"—With the cat on the table in either a sitting or standing position, show him the treat. Hold it just out of reach so he must hold out a paw to touch it—and give the command "Wave" as he does so. Give him the treat.

- "*Up*"—With the cat in a sitting position, hold the treat just out of reach directly above his head. Most cats will naturally stretch up and go into a begging position. When he does, give your command, and reward him with the treat.

Cat Nip: Naming New Commands

Choose a short, percussive-sounding word that begins with a consonant to identify any new action. It's easier for the cat to hear and to remember when it sounds different from any other command.

Learning Commands

Command Word	Behavior	Date First Learned
"Come"	Come to me when called	
"Sit"	Sit down	
"Wave"	Hold out your paw	
"Off"	Get off of or get down from	
"Up"	Stand up on your hind legs	

Cat Nip: Teaching New Behaviors

When you want your cat to perform a new behavior,
tempt him into the desired position with a treat. Identify
that behavior with a command. Each time your cat does the
desired behavior, repeat the command. Eventually your cat
will learn to associate the command with the behavior.

Kitty Corrections

NEVER HIT YOUR KITTEN OR CAT. Quite simply, it won't work. Cats do best with corrections that interrupt the behavior. Punishment after the misbehavior never works.

Identify corrections with a signal word like "No!" and use the signal word at the same time as you deliver the interrupting correction. Soon kitty learns to expect the correction whenever the word "No" is spoken.

Some effective cat corrections include:

- *Spray of water.* Use a long-distance squirt gun or plant sprayer, and aim for the tail—never squirt water into the cat's face.

- *Sudden noise.* Fill an empty soda can with some change, put tape over the opening, and shake it. Or slap a magazine against your hand.

- *Hissing like a cat.* A sudden, sharp "sssssssssst!!!" works especially well.

> ## Cat Nip: Sticky Paws
>
> *Use double-sided sticky tape on illegal scratching targets or forbidden counter-tops until kitty learns it's unpleasant to touch the surface—even when you aren't there to say "No!" A product called Sticky Paws™ works great.*

Always follow the correction by offering an opportunity to do the right thing. In other words, once the correction stops kitty from scratching the sofa, verbally praise him and move him to the legal scratch post. When he scratches in the right place, reward him.

PERSONALITY TRAITS

My cat refuses . . . .
. . . .
. . . .
. . . .
. . . .
. . . .
. . . .

When I give my cat a bath . . . .
. . . .
. . . .
. . . .
. . . .
. . . .
. . . .
. . . .
. . . .

A very strange thing my cat does is . . . .

. . . .

. . . .

. . . .

. . . .

. . . .

. . . .

My cat is afraid of . . . .

. . . .

. . . .

. . . .

. . . .

. . . .

. . . .

My cat drives me crazy when . . . .

. . . .

. . . .

. . . .

. . . .

. . . .

. . . .

EVERYDAY DELIGHTS

BEHAVIORS AND MANNERISMS

To get my attention my cat . . . .

. . . .

. . . .

. . . .

When I go to sleep my cat . . . .

. . . .

. . . .

. . . .

When my cat sees another cat . . . .

. . . .

. . . .

. . . .

When my cat sees a dog . . . .

. . . .

When my cat sees a bird . . . .

. . . .

. . . .

. . . .

. . . .

Cat Nip: Kitty Spies with Eyes

In relation to their body size, cats have the largest eyes of any mammal.

A really cute thing my cat does . . . .

. . . .

. . . .

When someone talks on the phone my cat . . . .

. . . .

. . . .

When someone comes over my cat . . . .

. . . .

. . . .

. . . .

Cat Nip: Greeting Houseguests

Usually it's best to let the kitten approach any house-guests. To avoid having a cat that is a shrinking violet or acts like he never met a stranger in his life, expose your kitten to a variety of different experiences and people early in his life. Doing this will increase the probability that your cat will be well adjusted when he gets older.

Tricks and Games

My cat's best tricks are . . . .
. . . .
. . . .
. . . .
. . . .

My cat loves to play . . . .
. . . .
. . . .
. . . .
. . . .

A great game that we made up is . . . .
. . . .
. . . .
. . . .
. . . .

Cat Nip: Going "Fishing" with Your Cat

Take an empty Kleenex® box and a sheet of tinfoil. Wad up the foil into a loose light ball, and drop it inside the box through the opening. Rattle the ball of foil around by shaking the box to show the kitty there's something inside; then stand back and watch kitty "fish" for the prize.

Exercising the Cat

KITTENS RACE AND RUN, climb and pounce their way through life. As kittens turn into cats, they begin to slow down a bit. Some cats may need encouragement to get off their furry tails.

The Benefits of Exercise

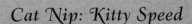

- It wears out high-energy cats. Cats given no constructive outlet for their energy will pester you to death and find all kinds of trouble to get into. Exercise channels energy and makes kitties more pleasant to be around.

- It keeps couch-potato kitties at a healthy weight. Indoor cats tend to sleep and eat a lot to combat boredom. Thin cats are healthier and live longer.

- It promotes bonding. Exercising can also eliminate some behavior problems.

Exercise Suggestions for Your Cat

- Chase games and tag to entice the cat to run up and down stairs

- Catch-it games with string-type or fishing-style toys or flashlight beams

- Ambush games with blankets where you hide the prize and let the cat find it

- Anything with catnip and climbing games on cat trees

Cat Nip: Kitty Speed

A domestic cat can sprint at about 31 miles per hour. Good luck if you try to win a footrace.

Favorite Cat Games

Playing Around

LIFE IS A GAME FOR KITTENS, and they spend lots of time and energy in play activities. This exercises not only their bodies but also their minds. Playing with your kitten is the most important way of bonding with each other. And besides, it's lots of fun!

Play Poses

- *Bunny Kick* Front paws grasp the "prey" or play object while the rear legs and claws bicycle against it and kick the stuffing out of it.

- *Stalk* The tail end goes up while the front end stays low, the rear paws "pedal" back and forth to get good traction, and the kitten rushes forward to capture the target.

- *Ambush* Cats love to hide behind objects or inside containers and catch you by surprise. People's ankles are often the target.

- *Mouse Pounce* Cats pounce—either by leaping in the air or raising up on their hind legs—to capture the toy with the front paws.

- *Bird Swat* Front paws bat objects out of the air. Kittens may leap straight up before swatting.

- *Fish Scoop* Cats love to "fish" in holes and see what they can scoop out. They use the technique to flip a toy out of a box or reach between sofa cushions to find buried treasure.

- *Tippy-Toe Sidle* Kittens often "pretend" to be scared when they play as an invitation to be chased. They stand high on their toes with the back arched and fur fluffed and almost tap-dance over the floor as they move sideways.

COMMERCIAL CAT TOYS

Interactive toys are ideal. Toys with string, feathers, or parts that can be easily pulled off and swallowed should only be used when you can watch your kitten. Some of the best choices are:

- Fishing-pole-style toys like the Galkie Kitty Tease
- Cat Dancer
- Plush soft toys
- Catnip-stuffed toys
- Cat Track
- Peacock or pheasant feather

CHEAP THRILLS

Cats tend to make their own fun and invent games using common household objects. Some of their favorites include:

- Empty box
- Paper bag
- Wadded paper or tinfoil
- Ping-pong ball in an empty Kleenex box or in the empty bathtub
- Bubbles
- Dripping water faucet
- Flashlight beam

Cat Nip: Play Behavior

Kittens begin to play at four weeks of age. The first display is on the back with paws waving— a defensive play-fight pose.

Cat's Favorites

Toys and friends . . . .
. . . .
. . . .
. . . .

Foods . . . .
. . . .
. . . .
. . . .

Places to hide . . . .
. . . .
. . . .
. . . .

Places to nap . . . .
. . . .
. . . .
. . . .
. . . .
. . . .

KITTY TREATS

KITTY BISCUIT TREATS

Mix together:
1¼ cups whole wheat flour
2 tbsp. wheat germ
4 tbsp. catnip
⅓ cup powdered milk

Stir together, then add to dry mix:
¼ cup milk + 1 tbsp.
2 tbsp. sesame oil
1 egg
2 tbsp. unsulphured molasses

Combine until the mixture forms a dough. Roll the dough into a thin sheet, and cut into various shapes. Place on a greased cookie sheet. Bake at 350° until lightly brown (about 20 minutes). Cool on rack to room temperature before offering to cat.

You can experiment with the recipe, too. Try substituting tuna juice from canned tuna (springwater-packed) for the ¼ cup milk. Or dice two or three raw shrimp, and add to the mixture prior to baking. Store biscuits in refrigerator. Use within 2 weeks or freeze.

KITTY LIVER COOKIES

1 lb. chicken liver
1 clove of garlic
1½ cups cornmeal
2 tbsp. wheat germ
2 eggs

1 tbsp. catnip (optional)
½ cup powdered milk
1 tbsp. brewer's yeast (optional)
2 tbsp. unsulphured molasses

Combine all ingredients in a food processor. Blend until smooth. Pour into greased pan. Cook at 375°, for 30 minutes. Cool completely before serving. Cut into small strips or shapes. Store in the refrigerator in an airtight container.

Cat Nip: Snacking Guidelines

It's not a good idea for kittens to receive too many treats because they need to get balanced, nutritious meals to fuel their growth.

KITTEN'S FIRST BIRTHDAY

TODAY . . . . , WE CELEBRATED

THE FIRST BIRTHDAY OF . . . . , OUR BELOVED CAT.

This joyous occasion was commemorated . . . .

. . . .

. . . .

. . . .

. . . .

. . . .

This event was shared with . . . .

. . . .

. . . .

. . . .

. . . .

. . . .

. . . .

. . . .

. . . .

. . . .

HAPPY BIRTHDAY

FIRST BIRTHDAY MEMORIES

BIRTHDAY MEMORIES

Holiday Warnings

WE OFTEN OVERLOOK THE POTENTIAL DANGERS of festive celebrations for our cats. Treat the safety of your cat just like you would treat that of a toddler during these events.

Guests

- Make sure guests know not to let the cat out if they aren't supposed to.

- Inform your guests not to feed the cat. They may inadvertently feed the cat something that can be toxic to him (e.g., onions or chocolate).

Gifts

- Gifts decorated with special trimmings and ribbons can pose a danger to your cat.

- Pick up gift wrapping soon after opening gifts.

Decorations

- A Christmas tree is an invitation to the cat to climb, so make sure the tree is stable. Make sure dangerous decorations aren't within kitty's reach. Beware—tinsel or icicles can be a deadly hazard if swallowed.

- Tack down or hide lights, cords, stockings, and garlands.

- Keep candles and menorahs out of the way of a curious nose or furry tail.

- Place an appropriate grill in front of the fireplace.

Festive Plants

- Be careful where you choose to display your holiday plants. Poinsettias, mistletoe, and holly are dangerous to your cat and can be fatal.

Food

- Make sure all the garbage is secure, and try not to leave food or candy within reach of the cat.

- When opening the oven or refrigerator, make sure a curious cat doesn't become trapped.

- Don't leave hot dishes where the cat can investigate them.

Cat Nip:
Kitty Christmas Tree

Consider having a "cat-safe" tree just for the kitten's enjoyment, perhaps decorated with catnip mice or other kitty toys.

FIRST HOLIDAYS

HOLIDAY MEMORIES

. . . .
. . . .
. . . .
. . . .
. . . .
. . . .
. . . .
. . . .
. . . .
. . . .
. . . .
. . . .
. . . .
. . . .
. . . .
. . . .
. . . .
. . . .
. . . .
. . . .
. . . .
. . . .
. . . .
. . . .
. . . .
. . . .
. . . .
. . . .
. . . .

HOLIDAY MOMENTS

Feline Fancies and Fantasies

If you could discover your cat's thoughts, what do you think they would be? . . . .

. . . .

. . . .

. . . .

What do you think your cat dreams about? . . . .

. . . .

. . . .

When I leave the house, my cat . . . .

. . . .

. . . .

My cat's perfect day would be spent . . . .

. . . .

. . . .

Cat Nip: Can Your Cat See in Color?

Cats are said to be able to see color.
Studies have proven that cats can
distinguish between red and green,
red and blue, green and blue,
blue and grey, and yellow and blue.

The Celebration of the Cat

Cats leave footprints on our hearts and we are never the same.
—Unknown

I am grateful for my cat . . . .

. . . .

. . . .

. . . .

. . . .

My cat reminds me to appreciate . . . .

. . . .

. . . .

. . . .

. . . .

The most important lesson I have learned . . . .

. . . .

. . . .

. . . .

. . . .

I have studied many philosophers and many cats.
The wisdom of cats is infinitely superior.
—Hippolyte-Adolphe Taine

MY CAT AND ME

Favorite Memories

REMEMBER WHEN

Traveling—or Not— with Your Cat

EVERY CAT MUST TRAVEL AT SOME POINT in his life, if only to visit the veterinarian or grooming shop. If you want to include your pet on family vacations, you'll need to make arrangements for the cat's comfort.

NECESSARY ITEMS

- *Carrier* Choose either a hard plastic carrier or a soft-sided bag. You must have an airline-approved hard case if you plan to ship your cat as cargo; there'll be an extra charge. Be sure to check the pet as "excess baggage" and not "freight" because freight may not travel on the same plane as you.

- *Health certificate and rabies certificate* These forms must accompany pets that travel across state lines or board airplanes.

- *Identification tag(s)* Ask your vet where to find these.

- *Food and water* Airlines require these if your pet travels as cargo. When traveling by car, it's best to provide the same food they're used to and to offer some ice to lick if they're thirsty (ice won't spill and make a mess).

CRATE TRAINING

- Turn the carrier into the cat's bed or a play area. Entice him into the carrier, shut the door for five or ten minutes, then release and praise. Do this several times a day for up to a week before the trip, and gradually increase the length of time the cat spends in the carrier.

- Make the carrier part of the furniture—don't bring it out only for trips. Otherwise, cats who only experience the carrier to ride to the vet for shots will hide whenever you bring it out.

- Once the cat is comfortable resting in the carrier, take him for short ten-minute rides in the car. When you return, let him out and give him a treat. Gradually extend the lengths of the ride.

> ## Cat Nip: A Cure for Car Sickness
>
> Cats don't often get carsick, but if yours does, try this ginger cure. Add a teaspoonful of fresh ginger to a cup of hot water to make a tea, let it cool, strain it, and add honey to taste. Then squirt 1/2 dropperful of the liquid into the cat's cheek—give about 20 minutes before traveling.

For long stays in the carrier, some cats do best if their vision is blocked, so drape a cloth over the grill. Cats that get very upset may benefit from tranquilizers; your veterinarian can recommend the right dose and medication. In almost every case, though, cats do better and are healthier traveling without being tranquilized.

STAYING AT HOME

- *Boarding* The best facilities are cat-only so that your pet doesn't become even more stressed by noisy dogs. You can request a referral from the American Boarding Kennels Association in Colorado Springs, 1-719-591-1113.

- *Pet sitters* The best, least stressful option for the cat is to stay in his home and have a care-taker come in one or more times a day. You can make arrangements to exchange this service with friends who have cats. There are also professional pet sitters. Request a referral from Pet Sitters International at 1-800-268-SITS.

ADVENTURES

Emergency Warning Signs

You are the first line of defense in your kitten's good health. It is vital that you learn to recognize normal cat behavior so you can get veterinary help promptly if something goes wrong. Kittens can't always tell us how they feel, and sometimes the signs are very subtle, so trust your instincts. Even if you can't put your finger on it, if something just doesn't feel right about the way the cat looks or acts, consult your veterinarian. The earlier an illness is caught and treated, the better the chance your kitten will fully recover.

Emergencies! See Veterinarian Immediately

- Fainting/loss of consciousness

- Hit by car

- Hypothermia (temperature below 96 degrees)

- Fall from high place

- Excessive bleeding/deep wounds

- Broken bone

- Straining with no result in litter box

- Burns

- Swallowed objects (string, thread, sharp objects)

- Electrical shock

- Vomiting or diarrhea for more than 36 hours

- Seizures

- Refusing to eat for more than 12 hours (for a kitten) or 36 hours (for an adult cat)

- Blood in urine, feces, or vomit

- Ingesting poisonous substances:

  Antifreeze

  Pest bait, or eating poisoned mice, etc.

  Insecticide (incorrectly applied flea products)

  Chocolate

SIGNS OF ILLNESS

- Dull coat

- Bald patches

- Continuous scratching

- Rash or sores

- Swelling anywhere

- Drinking a lot

- Urinating a lot

- Constipation

- Loss of appetite

- Diarrhea

- Discharge from the eyes, ears, or nose

- Lethargy

- Fever (temperature over 102 degrees)

- Vomiting

- Missing the litter box

- Coughing, wheezing, or sneezing

- Any sudden behavior change

- Worms in feces or vomit

Cat Nip: Rescue Stickers

To be better prepared for an emergency, such as a fire, earthquake, or flood, it is a very good idea to display an animal rescue sticker in a prominent place in your home. This way emergency personnel can see the sticker and be aware that there is a pet in the house.

Cat First Aid Kit

CREATING A FIRST AID KIT FOR YOUR PET is imperative, and it's simple to do. Make one for home and one for the car. Familiarize family members and anyone watching the cat with the kit and its location.

You can find first aid kits at pet supply stores, you can order them through catalogs, or you can create a kit yourself. It's important that the contents be clearly labeled, organized, and available at a moment's notice in one container. Any box will work, but a plastic storage container with a handle—like a sewing kit or tackle box—is ideal. Label it "Cat First Aid" in permanent marker. Tape important contact information, in permanent ink, to the inside lid:

- Your name, address, phone number, and e-mail address

- The name, address, and phone number of an emergency contact person

- The name, address, and phone number of your veterinarian

- The phone number of the Pet Poison Control hotline

For each cat that you have, make a card that includes his individual information:

- Cat's name, breed, description (e.g., black longhair, calico shorthair)

- Known health problems (e.g., diabetic, thyroid problems, prone to hairballs)

- Dosages for specific medicines in the kit

Before giving your cat any over-the-counter medication, check first with your veterinarian. Cats are very sensitive to certain ingredients and could be poisoned by drugs that are safe for people or dogs. Aspirin, Tylenol®, and ibuprofen (Advil®, Nuprin®, Motrin®, etc.) are dangerous to cats.

Fill in the dosage column with your veterinarian, and ask for any recommended additions to the kit.

Medicine/Equipment	Treatment for / Used for	Dosage (*consult vet for correct dosage)
Teaspoon and tablespoon	Measuring medicine	
Oral syringe	Dosing liquid medicine	
Pill syringe/dispenser	Administering pills	
Round-tip scissors	Cutting hair and bandages	
Rectal thermometer	Checking temperature	
Bulb syringe	Flushing wounds	
Pill cutter	Dosing medicine	
Betadine scrub	Using as antiseptic wash	
Triple antibiotic ointment	Dressing wounds	
Sterilized pads and tape	Covering wounds	
Instant cold pack	Reducing swelling	
Eye wash solution	Flushing eye injuries	
Tweezers	Removing foreign objects	
Cotton swabs and pads	Cleaning wounds	
Blanket or pillowcase	Restraining cat	
3% hydrogen peroxide*	Inducing vomiting	
Kaopectate®*	Controlling diarrhea	

HOMEMADE REMEDIES

IT'S ALWAYS BEST TO PARTNER with a veterinarian for the health care of your kitten. But often, a homemade remedy will work just as well as or even better than a prescription. In fact, more and more veterinarians are recommending a more natural approach to pet care and reserve drugs for very serious conditions.

Herbs work great when used correctly, but they can be just as dangerous as drugs and can potentially poison your kitten if you don't know what you're doing. There are also limits to what a homemade remedy can do. If the condition persists or gets worse, then a veterinary visit is needed.

Cat Nip: The Frozen Pea Trick

An ice pack works great to heal bruises and kill the pain of a strain or sprain. A bag of frozen peas is perfect because it molds to the cat's body.

Hairballs   To make a natural hairball remedy, combine raw oatmeal, honey, and olive oil into a paste. Offer one to two tablespoons whenever kitty has a problem. Most cats will eat this mixture like a treat; you can use it up to three times a week.

Bug Bites and Stings   Cats love to play with moving critters and may get stung in the process. Ammonia takes the pain away from bee stings and ant bites. Use a cotton swab, and dab the individual sores once a day.

Diarrhea   All kinds of serious illnesses cause diarrhea. Until you can get a veterinary diagnosis (which should be as soon as possible), give the cat some plain live-culture yogurt. When an upset stomach is the cause, yogurt can rebalance the bacteria inside the gut and calm down the diarrhea. Cats usually love the flavor, too. Give kittens one tablespoon a day spread over several small feedings.

Kitty Colds and Poor Appetite   Chicken soup seasoned with garlic has been shown to relieve congestion, fight infection, and tempt kitties to eat. That's because 1 milligram of the primary active ingredient found in garlic, called allicin, is equal in potency to 15 standard units of penicillin. Homemade soup is best, but canned soup seasoned with garlic works, too. You can give four to eight ounces of warm soup a day for up to three days.

Ear Mites   These tiny bugs live on the inside of kitty's ears and drive her mad with itching. Typically, you'll see black to brown crumbly debris inside the ears (it's best to get a veterinary diagnosis first). Studies have shown that using plain oil in the ears works just as well to cure the problem as using commercial products. Holistic vets recommend olive oil or almond oil, which are very healing to skin. Crush several cloves of garlic in ½ cup oil, and let soak overnight; the garlic fights bacterial infections. The next morning, strain out the garlic, so only the oil is left. Drip several drops into each ear, massage the base of the kitten's ears to spread the solution, then wipe out the excess with a cotton ball. You need to treat with this oil every day for at least a month to smother all the bugs.

Medical History

Veterinarian

Name. . . . .

Address . . . .

. . . .

Phone . . . .

Allergies

. . . .

. . . .

Neutered/Spayed

Date . . . .

Performed by . . . .

Cat Nip: Ensuring Kitty's Safety

Always make extra copies of the medical history, and leave with a neighbor, with the cat sitter, secured in kitty's carrier, and/or with the telephone emergency information. In case of a disaster, the information should be easily accessible to police, fire department, or other rescue personnel even if you aren't there to point it out.

MEDICAL RECORD CHART

DATE	PROBLEM	TREATMENT PRESCRIBED	VET

Medical Notes

VACCINATION RECORD

ON YOUR INITIAL VISIT TO YOUR VETERINARIAN, ask about the recommended schedule of vaccinations. Keeping your kitten's vaccinations up-to-date helps keep your cat as healthy as possible. Also, inquire about your town's or county's licensing requirements.

NAME OF VACCINE	PROTECTION AGAINST	DATE(S) ADMINISTERED	EXPIRATION DATE

IMPORTANT PHONE NUMBERS AND INFORMATION

ONCE YOU HAVE FILLED IN the information on the next page, make a photocopy of it, or type it into a computer document and print out the information. Tape this sheet of paper to your refrigerator. Make sure everyone knows where this information is located.

Cat Nip: Making a "Lost Cat" Sign

If your cat gets lost, first call local shelters to see if your cat was taken there. If necessary, make a "Lost Cat" sign and display it in as many places as you can, even in mailboxes. Make sure to: place a recent color picture of your cat on the sign; print the flyer on bright yellow paper with black ink; put the sign in a sheet protector if hanging outdoors. Include the following information: cat's name, age, and gender; owner's phone numbers and e-mail address (do not put any additional contact information); date lost; the location the cat was last seen; if you're offering a reward, say so but do not say how much.

Emergency Cat Information

Owner's Contact Information

Name . . . .

Address . . . .

. . . .

Phone . . . .

E-mail . . . .

Other Contact Information

Veterinarian (name and phone) . . . .

. . . .

Emergency contact (name and phone) . . . .

. . . .

ASPCA National Animal Poison Control Center:

1-800-548-2423 (charge on credit card)

1-900-680-0000 (charge to your phone bill)

Cat's Important Information

Call name . . . .

Breed . . . . Markings . . . .

Registration name (if any) . . . .

Registration number (if any) . . . .

Microchip ID number (if any) . . . .

RECOMMENDED BOOKS AND WEB SITES

FELINE READING LIST

HEALTH AND CARE

Cat Massage (St. Martin's Press) by Maryjean Ballner

New Choices in Natural Healing for Dogs & Cats (Rodale Press) by Amy D. Shojai

The Purina Encyclopedia of Cat Care (Ballantine) by Amy D. Shojai

Your Aging Cat (Howell Book House) by Kim Thornton

BEHAVIOR AND TRAINING

Competability: Building a Peaceable Kingdom Between Cats & Dogs (Three Rivers Press)
    by Amy D. Shojai

Is Your Cat Crazy? (MacMillan) by John C. Wright, Ph.D.

Psycho Kitty! (Penguin) by Pam Johnson Bennett

Shelter Cats (Howell Book House) by Karen Commings

GENERAL INTEREST

Cats for Dummies (IDG Books Worldwide) by Gina Spadafori and Paul Pion

Housecat; How to Keep Your Indoor Cat Sane and Sound (IDG Books Worldwide) by Christine Church

FELINE WEB SITES

American Veterinary Medical Association	www.avma.org
American Holistic Veterinary Medical Association	www.altvetmed.com
American Association of Cat Enthusiasts (AACE)	www.aaceinc.org
American Animal Hospital Association	www.healthypet.com
American Cat Fanciers Association (ACFA)	www.acfacat.com
Cat Fanciers' Association, Inc. (CFA)	www.cfainc.org
Cat Fanciers Federation (CFF)	www.cffinc.org
Alley Cat Allies	www.alleycat.org

Pet Supply Catalogs

Name	Telephone Number	Web Site
Arcata Pet	1-800-822-9085	www.arcatapet-online.com
Care A Lot	1-800-343-7680	www.carealot.org
Cat Faeries	1-415-585-6400	www.catfaeries.com
Doctors Foster & Smith	1-800-826-7206	www.drsfostersmith.com
Fat Cat, Inc.	1-802-655-1300	www.kittyhoots.com
Jeffers	1-800-533-3377	www.jefferspet.com
New England Serum Co.	1-800-637-3786	www.NESerum.com
Noah's Pet Supplies	1-888-NOAHS PET	www.noahspets.com
Omaha Vaccine	1-800-367-4444	www.omahavaccine.com
Pedigrees	1-800-548-4786	n/a
Petopia	1-877-PETOPIA	www.petopia.com
Pets.com	1-888-321-7387	www.pets.com
Pet Warehouse	1-800-443-1160	www.petwhse.com
R. C. Steele	1-800-872-3773	www.rcsteele.com

In Loving Memory

It is in celebration of the life of

. . . .

that I record and honor the cherished memories
and knowledge gained by knowing such a great being.
Our wonderful journey began on

. . . .

And today

. . . .

marks the day that my friend
leaves this world for another.

A MEMORIAL TRIBUTE

Some of the wisdom that I gained from knowing . . . .
. . . .
. . . .
. . . .
. . . .

My most cherished memories . . . .
. . . .
. . . .
. . . .
. . . .
. . . .
. . . .
. . . .
. . . .
. . . .

I believe cats to be spirits come to earth
A cat, I am sure
Could walk on a cloud without coming through.

—JULES VERNE

About the Authors

Lorie Glantz has shared her life with animals for over 20 years. Currently, she resides in Burlington, Massachusetts, with her husband, son, and Golden Retriever. She is also the author of *My Dog's Tale*. For more information about enriching your life with your cat, or to contact Lorie, go to www.mycatstale.com.

Amy D. Shojai is a nationally known authority on pet care and behavior. She is the author of 14 nonfiction pet books and more than 300 published articles and columns. She is also the spokesperson for Purina brand pet foods and the founder and president of the international Cat Writers' Association. She appears regularly on national radio and television programs in connection with her pet writing. She travels extensively to lecture on proper pet care and can be reached at www.shojai.com. Ms. Shojai is happy to answer kitten and cat care questions.

About the Illustrator

Emily Youngreen is an artist with over 30 years of experience in illustration, oil painting, watercolor, and more. She has recently completed *When Mommy Sings to the Forest,* a moving and mystical children's book. She currently lives in British Columbia, Canada.